THE HERITAGE OF
ENGLAND
IN COLOUR

THE HERITAGE OF ENGLAND IN COLOUR

A Collection of Colour Photographs by

A. F. KERSTING

With an Introductory Text and Notes on the Illustrations by

JOHN BLEDLOW

LONDON
B. T. BATSFORD LTD

First published 1956

PRINTED AND BOUND IN GREAT BRITAIN
BY JARROLD AND SONS LTD, LONDON AND NORWICH
FOR THE PUBLISHERS
B. T. BATSFORD LTD
4 FITZHARDINGE STREET PORTMAN SQUARE LONDON W1

CONTENTS

LIST OF ILLUSTRATIONS

I Community Heirlooms

I SHOULD like to begin by drawing attention to the title of the book and make a short stand on the word "heritage". It has become a much-used word and, to take a line from the pen of Walter Scott, "use lessens marvel". Yet this heritage of ours is indeed something to marvel at! In architecture alone, we of the twentieth century are born to a great inheritance of works which sometimes took more than a single lifetime to create, the product of earnest and devoted minds working through the hands of men skilled by the practice of generations of craftsmanship. They were completed early and late in our history, and now some are only ruinous fragments of what they were; even so, they are more than mere reminders of the past, for they challenge the imagination to restore them to their former selves and to surround them with the life they once knew.

The continuity of our national history has been of such a happy sort that no political upheaval or enemy invasion of our soil has made a serious break with the past since the Norman Conquest of 1066. We have passed from feudalism to free democracy, from absolute to constitutional monarchy in civil affairs, and in religious matters from the supremacy of Rome to native Church government and complete tolerance of all forms of worship. The Reformation, the Renaissance movement, and the Civil War of 1640 were crises which produced radical changes in outlook, in architectural fashion, and indeed some regrettable damage to fine buildings. But they were not sufficient to break the thread of national continuity or the long entail of our architectural inheritance.

And so we have in our countryside memorials in stone and wood of every principal phase of the reactions of our people in the course of those nine centuries. Before the great break of the Norman Conquest there are indeed links with the doings of more than three thousand earlier years, one of which forms the subject of our first picture.

II Assessment

THE valuation of an ordinary private inheritance is assessed in terms of cash by a professional valuer who has a fair idea of what a thing would fetch in the open market. But the sort of heritage which forms the subject of this book cannot be measured by material standards. Its value lies in its appeal to the imagination through the visual expression of art and charm, through association with men and events of earlier days, and as witnessing to purposes which once formed the framework of institutions—

some decayed, some persisting—on which our own present-day structure is founded.

My purpose here, then, is to attempt to give some indication of the variety of this great inheritance and of its worth in those abstract values just mentioned; also a rough key to the kind and nature of the subjects from which Mr. Kersting has selected his favourites to present in the following picture-gallery.

III Houses, Mansions, and Palaces

THE big old house in the country and the entrance lobby in the little modern house in the town are each entitled to call themselves the *hall* by virtue of a common descent from one ancestor. This was the mediaeval hall, a one-roomed house of an almost standard design. As the home of a family sufficiently well-to-do to have retainers and servants it consisted of a large oblong building resembling the nave of a church and, like it, open to the rafters. The floor at one end was slightly raised to form a dais and mark a definite social boundary. This was the *upper* end of the hall and on this dais the master of the house, his family, and particular guests sat at table.

The entrance was near the end of the lower hall where there was usually a door on either side, opening alternately on the front approach and on the garden. To give protection from the draught of these doors a wooden partition (usually of well-carved wainscot) was placed across the room forming a passage between doors, called the *screens*. Walking through this passage you would then have on the one hand the door, or pair of doors, leading through the partition into the hall, on the other, three archways for the buttery hatch (whence came the drinks), the kitchen, and the pantry. This passage of the screens usually carried a low ceiling which was made use of as the floor of a minstrel's gallery.

The hall could be, and usually was, all-sufficing as the complete house, acting as dining-room and common-room during the day and dormitory by night. Tables were of the trestle variety, at least in the lower hall, and easily dismantled, beds were of the very simplest:

The tables were drawn, it was idlesse all;
Knight, and page, and household squire,
Loiter'd through the lofty hall
Or crowded round the ample fire;

The stag-hounds, weary with the chase,
Lay stretch'd upon the rushy floor,
And urged, in dreams, the forest race,
From Teviot-stone to Eskdale-moor.

This "ample fire" was kindled in a large brazier in the centre of the hall, its smoke and fumes rising to the ridge of the roof, where they escaped through a small turret with open slats, called a *louver*. It was generally topped by a weather-cock and made a picturesque addition to the look of the hall when seen from outside.

The more important halls had a small room annexed which might be described as a bed-sitting-room for the lord and his lady called the *solar*. Everyone else, including distinguished guests, had to make do in the hall. In the "private" house, privacy was not a thing that had yet begun to matter; it showed signs of doing so in the fourteenth and fifteenth centuries, but not until the sixteenth did the real break with tradition come and the hall begin to be only part of the house instead of the whole of it.

Owing largely to the redistribution of wealth and land after the Reformation and the introduction of Italian ideas, there was a tremendous output of new housing for "new men" between the middle and end of the sixteenth century. It was marked by quite revolutionary features—upper floors, grand staircases, more rooms.

Many new houses retained the hall much as it was, but now as a ground-floor room only, with a storey added above, reached by a broad staircase with landing and carved newels and banisters. Where formerly there had been nothing between floor and open roof, the latter was now made use of as an attic storey, lit by a row of gabled windows. Many older halls were adapted to follow this arrangement. That meant the abandonment of the time-honoured central-heater—the brazier—for wall-fireplaces (soon to prove a new focal point for decoration and house-pride). The insertion of these floors produced another new feature, the plaster ceiling, which immediately became a field for decoration in relief. Additional accommodation was provided by adding wings at right angles to either end of the main building, those at the *upper* end of the hall for the family, those at the lower end for the servants—this was the *servants' hall*, a term which, like the other, long outlived any resemblance to its original self and, in London houses of the eighteenth and early nineteenth century, occupied the basement. The porch, which had been a feature of the simple hall was now the central feature of the main building and carried up through one storey or to the roof level as an oriel window. This, with the wings, produced a letter "E" in plan, which started the old antiquarian rumour that the design was a pretty compliment to Queen Elizabeth.

Many older halls adapted themselves in more or less degree to the new fashion of roominess and the withdrawal from each other of the social grades, a distinction that was steadily growing more and more marked as the use of the single common living-room receded into the past.

But the hall-house was not the only one in process of evolution; there was the fortified manor-house. This was mainly a product of the fourteenth century, and remaining examples show that it followed the plan of the castles which were beginning to be built in the early years of that century, or just a little earlier. It was more house than castle but still capable of being put into a state of defence and, on that account, had to be granted a licence "to crenellate" (*i.e.* make use of battlements and loopholes) by the king.

These houses took the form of an enclosed courtyard (or two courts) within a moat, having an imposing gatehouse with drawbridge and usually a tower mounting battlements at one angle of the court, but they were only lightly fortified to withstand a Border raid or an attack from armed bandits. In such a manor-house the inevitable hall would still be there, forming one side of the court, but in the remaining three there was much more room for privacy and separate establishments. The ruined Wingfield Manor in Derbyshire is a fine and typical example. Early in the Tudor period this type of house was being built without any serious consideration of the "security" side, towers and gatehouses being retained as purely picturesque features, their battlements replaced by leaden cupolas, surmounted by gilded weathercocks. One of the earliest and most ambitious works of the kind was Hampton Court, begun by Cardinal Wolsey in 1515, a house where 280 separate apartments were kept furnished ready for expected guests and the household staff was nearly 500 persons.

Towers and gatehouses in their innocent mock-fortress forms were most attractive to the novelty-loving people of Tudor England. They liked to make "my poore house" look as much like the palace of a Fairie Queene as possible, a background for the parade of stuffed doublets, slashed trunk-hose, and well-goffered ruffs.

About the beginning of the seventeenth century when the lightsome Elizabethan style merged into the more solemn Jacobean manner there was a general interchange of ideas between the (unfortified) courtyard house and the "E" house; the latter was often built with extended wings so as to form a three-sided court and given a moat and gatehouse that were purely ornamental. Rushton Hall in Northamptonshire, which has an open stone screen enclosing the fourth side of the court, shows one form of the compromise well, An interesting and very splendid example of conversion of "E"-to-courtyard house is Burleigh, near Stamford, the home of

Elizabeth's great Chancellor, built near the end of the sixteenth century. It may be contrasted with one of the latest and greatest courtyard houses begun in the first year of the Jacobean Age (1603), Audley End (p. 95).

Of the smaller manor-houses, Mr. Kersting has selected an interesting one, the seat of the lord of Brockhampton manor in the fourteenth century (p. 93). It is a simple hall-house of that time built in half-timber to which a single wing has been added in the roomier days and also an unfortified gatehouse, as a picturesque amenity (with room over) which also acts as a bridge over the moat. The original hall is still there. This is a moated manor-house but not one that was ever fortified (within the meaning of that rule). One could cast a moat about a house without having to apply for a licence to crenellate. The Ordnance map notes the site of hundreds of moated homesteads all over the country only indicated now by a grass-grown fosse, or the vestige of one, from which the wooden home has long since disappeared even from memory. There was probably no military intention in this light defence but something to damp the ardour of the outlaw or the unpaid ex-soldier turned robber.

The eighteenth century was the great age of mansions and if, for once, one might use the term "mansion" in a special sense, I would here wish it to mean the great solid four-square block of a house which was the logical follower of the courtyard type, crystallised and compressed, sometimes showing its ancestry by a small "area" in the middle to give light, sometimes a similar space glassed over by a dome or skylight above the well of a main staircase with its landings.

By now architects had come to take the classical implications of the Renaissance much more seriously than the fancy-free Elizabethans. Anglicised versions of Vitruvius and Palladio were available laying down unbreakable rules about proportion and balance and though people like Wren and Vanbrugh could take a high-handed line with these august instructors and play tricks not laid down in their manuals the more pedestrian builder did his best to obey orders. Their ideas of well-proportioned openings were greatly assisted by the invention of the sash window in place of that filled with stone mullions. But a leading feature of the "E" house had a come-back in a "proper" Italianate disguise. Its wings had been rectangular and entirely utilitarian. In the new form the wings became mere antennae, curving gracefully in half-moons to right and left, colonnaded loggias, ending in small block-like buildings called pavilions. These served no utilitarian purpose in the domestic economy of the house (often quite the reverse). Their intention was purely optical, to "balance" the solid block-like mass of the house itself. A development of this plan on the colossal scale is seen at Blenheim Palace where, indeed, the pavilions are mansions in themselves.

This age, which began with the resounding victories of Marlborough and ended with disasters in America and the Napoleonic War, saw the culmination of house-building in England when the "big house" had become so much bigger that it had entirely outgrown its domestic character and could only be thought of as a palace. Grandeur took first place, comfort was hardly considered at all. The gulf which had separated master and servant since the days of the common hall had become great and impassible. The nobleman, like the Roman Emperor, whose re-created forms surrounded him, esteemed his "worth and birth" as something superhuman and received his privileged inferiors in a "presence-chamber". Such house-pride, however, promoted lavish patronage. Under it architects, sculptors, and painters throve as never before or since and their foregathered works in these great residences, preserved in so many instances from dispersal by the National Trust, have become one of the most valuable parts of the English heritage.

IV Castles

THE development of the English castle (in which the domestic side played its part as well as military necessity) followed rather similar lines to that of the ordinary private residence and sometimes led the way. Castles are recorded as having existed in Saxon England but they appear to have been simple defence-works of earthern bank-and-palisade and no recognisable remains have been discovered. The Normans introduced a type called motte-and-bailey which, in its simplest form consisted of a high mound of earth—the motte—on which a wooden tower was erected. To it was attached an oval enclosure—the bailey—cast about by a moat whose excavation supplied material for a breastwork surmounted by a wooden palisade.

This simple and effective work could be quickly run up in a mobile campaign—William's second castle at York (1069) is said to have been completed within eight days. It was equally sound as the basis for a permanent structure and, with a few exceptions, all our castles founded in the eleventh and twelfth centuries were begun on this plan, the wooden work of the tower and palisade being later replaced by stone. The exceptions I have mentioned were not in actual plan but through having the great tower, or *keep*, built in stone from the beginning. The strength and height of such a building made the artificial mound unnecessary. It is these large stone keeps which have resisted so successfully the sieges of man and time, that best preserve the framework of living conditions in the eleventh and twelfth centuries and, by extraordinary good luck, the very first of them to be made, the Tower of London, has come down to us, with fabric, floors, and roof, in perfect repair. Built by the Conqueror almost immediately after Hastings and completed in his successor's reign, it is scarcely altered except for the Tudor cupolas capping the turrets and some window widening by Sir Christopher Wren. The only important detail missing is the forebuilding, an embattled staircase giving access to the main entrance on the first floor, a regular feature of the stone keeps rising from level ground and of which a perfect example survives at the keep in Newcastle-upon-Tyne.

The Tower was a royal residence as well as a fortress and had to provide accommodation for a retinue of servants, officials, and clerks, as well as the garrison. Even so, there was more opportunity for segregation and privacy than in the hall-house, as the building was divided horizontally into floors (three floors and a basement) and vertically by a main cross-wall. In addition, there were, in several of these large keeps, sleeping chambers contrived in the thickness of the wall. In the Tower, the great hall occupied the second floor and a fine chapel with aisles, triforium gallery, and rounded apse adjoined it. Only one other keep on exactly the same plan, though even larger in dimension, was ever built, that at Colchester, a contemporary work (eleventh century).

In the bailey, which was nearly always a two-fold enclosure—inner and outer—there would, in addition, be wooden buildings, stabling, etc., as required, and in the plain motte-and-bailey fort, where accommodation in the wooden tower must have been limited to the principal residents and men-at-arms on guard, there would be a great hall in the inner bailey where similar arrangements for eating and sleeping would prevail as in the hall of a civilian.

Before passing on to the next great change, which came early in the thirteenth century, it should be observed that castles were built and held by three different sections of the community. Besides the royal castles, widely distributed throughout the realm, there were those of the barons, also fairly widely distributed as, for political reasons, the Conqueror had chosen to grant fiefs to his more powerful followers in regions which did not adjoin each other; thirdly, there were the castles of the bishops within their own dioceses.

The bishops' castles tended to be more ornate than the others for, being presumed men of peace (though they occasionally took the field in armour) and patrons of the arts, their castles were generally distinguished by architectural excellence—as may be seen at Acton Burnell, St. Davids, and Wells. The mediaeval bishop, besides being a spiritual lord, was also a territorial baron, and to have a fortified house was an outward and visible sign of that state; in the borders of Wales and Scotland and a few other places it was a necessity. But the reason why each bishop had several castles or plain manor-houses was that, in order to administer the extensive area of his diocese, for confirmations, ordinations, consecrations, and other business which he could not transact by proxy, he had to move continually from district to district with an enormous retinue of clerks, lawyers, and servants who would consume all the available supplies on each manor in turn, which the limited agricultural ingenuity of those days had been able to produce each year.

There was an important development in castle-building in the first quarter of the thirteenth century, another in the last quarter. In the former, the wooden palisade defences of the bailey were replaced with stone curtain-walls from which half-round towers projected, pierced with loop-holes, from which bow-shot could sweep the intervals between them. The entrance was contrived between two larger towers of the same kind, called drum-towers. Few new castles were built, and those which were renovated followed closely, as a rule, the old line of inner and outer bailey (now called *wards*); the keep was retained as a last defence strong-point and not materially altered (Chepstow is an outstanding exception).

The second change came at the end of the Welsh wars of Edward I when a series of brand new castles were built by a king who had personally been to Syria as an active Crusader and inspected the latest product of French and Byzantine ingenuity in the art of fortress engineering. All Edward's castles in Wales show a progressive series of experiments during which the keep was abandoned and a large roomy gatehouse with comfortable quarters for the castellan was made the strongest point and last resort in the castle's defence. In the second place, the mural towers were made not only units in the defence of the wall but habitable dwellings for officials or chief members of the garrison. In the third place, the traditional plan of having two wards (or baileys) adjoining each other was radically revised in favour of placing one within the other, an outer ring with curtain and towers of moderate height, and an inner ring, stronger and higher, to continue resistance if the outer fell.

These castles had many lean-to wooden buildings in the wards but the great hall was a substantial and handsome apartment of stone with large traceried windows on the side of the court. Yet there was still a relic of motte-and-bailey tradition in the arrangement of having an assortment of detached buildings dotted about in the open wards. The plan was at last pulled together about half-way through the long reign of Edward III when what is generally called the courtyard type of castle emerged (not at all a good name!). The leading feature of these castles was that the buildings were conterminous. They were grouped round a four-sided courtyard in four consolidated ranges, and with a large tower at each corner. The ranges were of more than one storey and there was a continuous roof-line just below the wall-walk of the battlements interrupted only by the towers.

This was the last development of the castle within the mediaeval period, when weapons of siege and defence were still predominantly mechanical and explosives were in their infancy, a development nearly all in the direction of home comforts. Two very fine specimens of the courtyard castle have survived at Bodiam in the south and Wensleydale in the north. The former (p. 61) is on the left bank of the River Rother which seems to have been navigable by vessels of shallow draught in the fourteenth century and on that account a possible source of danger from an enemy raid if ships succeeded in penetrating the defences of the cinque port, Rye,* at its mouth. On that plea, Sir Edward Dalyngrigge, who had acquired the manor of Bodiam by marriage, applied for a licence to crenellate. This being granted by Richard II in 1385, he proceeded not merely to fortify his manor-house but to build a brand new castle with all the traditional embattlement (dungeon included), combined with the latest amenities in house-room. The castle is a plain rectangle (45 yards by 52) with a large round tower, topped by a turret, at each corner, a square one mid-way on either side, a strong gatehouse, heavily machicolated and displaying armorial bearing on the north front, with a strong postern facing south. It is surrounded by an artificial lake where now water-lilies flourish and wild-fowl make their home.

Castle Bolton, at the entrance to Wensleydale in the Yorkshire Pennines, can be dated just six years earlier than Bodiam. It is similar in plan but more severe in appearance, having large square towers at the corners instead of round ones and a very plain entrance. But, while Bodiam is a mere shell, Castle Bolton still retains one of its four ranges of courtyard buildings, complete with all floors and interior arrangements, and it was in this part of the castle that Mary, Queen of Scots, spent her first term of imprisonment in 1568, for the owner of the castle, Lord Scrope, happened to be Governer of Carlisle at the time when Mary crossed the Solway in the hope of a more sympathetic reception in England. The rooms which she occupied are still floored and ceiled and seem faintly redolent of the presence of that tragic queen.

When Charles I ascended the throne in 1625, the security of the realm from foreign foes, Border raiders, and noble faction-leaders, must have seemed so well assured for all time as to make castles appear outmoded superfluities, relics of a barbaric age and quite intolerable as houses. Then, in less than a score of years, there broke out the struggle between King and

* Rye was, in fact, raided and burnt by a French force in 1386.

Parliament and a twenty-six-year war ensued in which nearly all the castles were resorted to once more and though "stormed at by shot and shell" (for which they were never built) held out with surprising stoutness, though suffering great harm to their future value for the antiquary. But much worse was yet to happen to them; for, when the Royalist cause was lost, the triumphant Parliament sent demolition parties the round of them with orders to damage them by blowing such large gaps in their old defences that they were no longer of any military value.

No doubt if this most unfortunate of all our wars had been avoided our heritage of mediaeval castles would have been much richer and more complete. Of those remaining to us (barring the Tower of London), Ludlow Castle (p. 49) has perhaps the most varied range of interesting points both for the antiquary and the romantic of any. Begun in the eleventh century, it was occupied continuously until the end of the seventeenth, and can show work of every period. For long it was one of the key fortresses on the Welsh Border, owned not by the crown but the most powerful of the marcher baron families, the Mortimers, and probably its most exciting days were those of the Wars of the Roses when the head of the house was the Yorkist claimant to the throne. When that claimant was successfully crowned as Edward IV it became, automatically, a royal castle. Later, under the Tudors, it occupied a unique role. While retaining its garrison and its military power, it became the seat of the court set up under the English Prince of Wales to maintain law and order in the Principality, the old headstrong marcher baronies, and the four English Border counties. This Council for Wales and the Marches sat under a Lord President whose residency was in the castle.

The Council was not dissolved until the reign of William III, and all the buildings, old and new, were intact until the middle of the eighteenth century, when the lead was stripped off the large area of roofs and the timbers allowed to rot from exposure to the weather. As a shell, however, it is practically complete in every part, to the full height of its walls. Every castle had its chapel. That at Ludlow was a full-sized church, built detached in the inner ward in the twelfth century, one of a particular type thought to have been modelled on that of the Holy Sepulchre at Jerusalem —a round church, such as can still be seen at Cambridge and the Temple in London.

In point of preservation and the number of different building periods to be observed, Ludlow could be compared with Dover, though here the keep is more than half a century later than that at Ludlow. Dover Castle (p. 57) has also a full-sized church as garrison chapel—older than anything at Ludlow, for it is a Saxon work. Ludlow has three wards, two laid out in the eleventh century, the third in the twelfth, all standing on the original lines of the motte-and-bailey plan (in this case the stone tower taking the place of the motte). The concentric element of the ward-within-ward was never introduced. Dover, however, managed to make the best of both these worlds of the twelfth and thirteenth centuries, largely due to the nature of the ground which favoured first one plan and then the other. Dover can boast the longest stretch of "period" building of any; for there stands within its outer ward a Roman lighthouse which is believed to belong to the very early years of the Occupation—its claim to be "the first building in England" has not been seriously damaged by any debunker—and the tale ends by additions and reinforcements against an invasion by Napoleon in the early nineteenth century.

The great castle-palace of Windsor (p. 59) is in a class by itself. The site was chosen by William the Conqueror (exactly why so far from London is not quite clear) and work proceeded with about the same time as the Tower. The motte-and-bailey plan, as then drawn, has never been altered. But the motte, a natural chalk excrescence, was scarped to shape and not "made". On it William built a circular enclosing-wall of stone, which has hardly the height to be called a shell-keep, such as was built a century later and is more like the old Gaelic rath or cashel. It must have contained a wooden tower such as usually crowned the routine motte but one infinitely more secure by virtue of the outer wall of stone which however closely beset could not be breeched by fire. In Henry II's time, when the shell-keep had come into fashion, a great tower of this kind was built within William's wall, and so closely fitting that it rose flush with the old wall-walk which then formed a parapet ten feet wide between the two walls.

This circular keep is the dominant feature of all distant views of the castle and representations of it on biscuit-boxes, tea-caddies, and other "suitable gifts". But it was left to George IV and his architect, Wyatville, to give it the real biscuit-box finish. This they did in 1826 by adding another 33 feet to the height of the great tower with an oversailing battlement bristling with machicoulis, and surmounting the whole by a turret for display of the royal standard. In fact, all the most imposing parts of Windsor Castle, except St. George's Chapel, are renovations or complete novelties of Wyatville. For Charles II, finding the place dark and uncomfortable as a royal residence, had done away with as much mediaevalism as he could and remodelled it (as cheaply as possible) in a plain neo-classical style, so that it looked more like a barracks than a castle. But George IV wanted it made the most romantic-looking of any castle in his realm, and it was given to Wyatville to re-mediaevalise both the royal apartments and the fortifications.

After the honourable buffets and dishonourable slightings of the Civil

War very few castles, in whole or in part, were fit to live in, though there were few exceptions, Ludlow being one. There remained, however, a utilitarian purpose they might fulfil, and a great many were made to do so. That was to act as local gaols where neither comfort nor proof against damp were matters of moment; their absence was rather a recommendation to the justices of the eighteenth century. The building of official prisons removed even this last vestige of human care from the proud relics of the feudal age. Yet it was their very mouldering which stirred the romantic fancy of the Gothic revivalists, and the last fruits of this powerful movement were the formation and incorporation of the National Trust in 1907 and the promotion of the Ancient Monuments Act in 1913. By these means they have entered a new and quite unlooked for phase of peaceful reparation. Their ruins have been re-enobled as part of the national heritage.

V Wooden Walls

CASTLES, although abandoned and neglected, do not disappear unless overtaken by some quite exceptional circumstance such as that which happened to the great and historic Edwardian fortress of the town of Berwick-upon-Tweed and the strong castle of Northampton, each completely demolished in the mid-nineteenth century to make room for a railway station. But those "wooden walls" which have, in fact, played a more active and decisive part in defending us from the aggression of foreign powers have vanished altogether or left but a bare legacy in the shape of a figure-head or a ship's bell,

But there is one exception. It is no small achievement to have succeeded in preserving and restoring a great man-of-war of the days of sail as part of our heritage, and that ship the most famous in the annals of the Royal Navy—H.M.S. *Victory*. So her picture appears on page 65 as a tail-piece to the story of our bulwarks in stone which the poet Campbell rated as of quite secondary importance to those of wood:

Britannia needs no bulwark,
No towers along the steep;

The *Victory* is indeed a treasure both of archaeological and sentimental value, an epitome of the old hard-won sea-skill, the practical and symbolic embodiment of something gradually moulded by the hands of many old masters—shipmen of the Cinque Ports, Elizabethan captains, shipwrights of the Pepysian era and the Anson revival.

VI Churches and Monasteries

IN these days when we speak of "the Government" we think first of Whitehall and the chiefs in power at Westminster and perhaps give a second thought to the offices of local government. We hardly think of the bishops, although they still have seats in the upper House and contribute in no small degree to debates on governmental measures. It was a very different state of affairs in the Middle Ages. There was indeed a central government at the court of the king (of which Parliament formed a part). Here, the Church had a large say, and the chancellor, chief minister of the crown, was often a high ecclesiastic. Local government was partly a matter for the bishops in their dioceses, and there was an ecclesiastical court to reckon with as well as a civil court. The religious houses played a part in both national and local government, the heads of the greater ones were compelled to assume the responsibilities and functions of territorial lords, and the houses themselves vied with the schools as chief training centres for administrators. For long after the Reformation, when the civil power had become paramount, parishes were still largely governed by the vestry-meeting on which the squire sat but the parish priest presided and the church-wardens were principal members. They managed the rates and elected the village constable.

The Church, as much a living moral force as it ever was, has been freed from most of the civil obligations with which the feudal regime loaded it but, in assessing the sentimental and historical value of the older buildings of religion, many of which though much ruined we now cherish, their great contribution to the good government of the realm should not be forgotten while apprising their architectural and aesthetic points. A close reading of history shows clearly that the foundations of our boasted democracy were first laid within these sacred precincts.

Of religious buildings there are four principal kinds, parish churches, collegiate churches, cathedrals, and monasteries. Taken as a whole, and reckoning their vast number and great variety, their intimate contact with every class of the population down the ages, and their sustained influence for the maintenance of the Christian principle throughout that time, our parish churches must surely be the most valuable part of our heritage. But their very diversity makes them too formidable a subject to treat within the scope of the present book.

The term collegiate church is a loose one. It simply means the church of a religious community and can therefore apply to both the cathedral and the monastic church. It holds good equally for a church no bigger than a parish church but built to be served by a small college (or community) of priests. A typical instance is Battlefield Church near Shrewsbury, an early war-memorial. It was built on the site of Henry IV's victory over the forces assembled under Harry Hotspur and other leading opponents of the first Lancastrian king, the founders being the rector of the parish where the battle took place and the King (whose image still stands over the east window). It was endowed for the support of a master and five chaplains who were to pray perpetually for the souls of the slain. The building completed about 1408 (bar the tower) is about the size of an average village church. But no parochial rights were attached to it until long after its foundation and, before restoration, it appears to have lacked the usual division between nave and chancel. It was simply a *choir* for this small college of priests to sing their services in.

A cathedral is collegiate, in that it contains a choir for a college of another sort, in this case for the chapter, which is the governing body of the diocese, under the bishop. England is peculiar in having two kinds of cathedral chapter, one secular, the other monastic. There is, I think only one instance of the monastic cathedral on the Continent, namely at Monreale in Sicily. It serves the double purpose of the church of a monastery and the seat of the bishop. Its choir is therefore of great size, as it has to provide seating for all the monks as well, as the higher officials of the diocese will probably be secular clergy but not monks. The bishop, though seldom a monk himself, was given the courtesy title of abbot, but his chapter was ruled by the prior of the monastery, an arrangement which was frequently a cause of much clerical friction.

In the secular cathedral the chapter was composed of secular canons (clergy not under monastic vows). They lived in houses of their own in the cathedral close and had separate incomes derived from rectories in the countryside. Unlike the monks, they were only obliged to be in residence in the cathedral precinct for a short period of the year, their place in the choir for singing the seven daily services being taken by men which they fee'd from their own purse for the purpose, called vicars choral. Arrangements for housing these "singing men" varied from place to place and cannot always be traced. At Exeter they occupied a common establishment which remained intact until destroyed by bombs in the 1939-1945 war. At Wells they were more amply provided for with a common hall adjoining the cathedral, and a quadrangle of small dwellings called the Vicars' Close. Both these remain intact although there have been no vicars choral for four centuries. The Vicars' Hall, approached from the choir by a flight of steps and a bridge is one of the most picturesque buildings in the old city.

The cathedral, itself, while being a collegiate church, is distinguished from all others as having within it the *cathedra* or bishop's chair (now generally called his *throne*, though a three-legged stool for episcopal use would still confer cathedral rank on the building). At the Reformation, when all the monasteries were dissolved, the monastic cathedrals were given secular chapters; the old monastic precinct then became the close, and the new incoming canons made the best use they could of the conventual buildings as private houses, pulling down what was unsuitable, for the stone afforded, and letting the remainder fall into ruin. In nearly all cases, however, the cloister and chapter-house, opening out of it, were preserved. The latter was naturally as essential to the new regime as it had been to the old, and the cloister was a feature that the secular cathedrals had copied from the monasteries for though, unlike the monks, they had no real use for this covered gallery, they seem to have thought it one of the "extras" which a great church ought to possess to add to its dignity. Thus, at Salisbury, which has always been a secular cathedral, there is an immense cloister which has not even the excuse of serving the purpose of a covered walk in rainy weather as there is a wide gap between the end of it and the house of any dignitary of the cathedral.

Just as it was expected of the commander-in-chief to live in the handsomest pavilion in the field, so it was expected of the mediaeval bishop that both his church and his palace should be given all architectural stateliness and all the "extras". These may be counted as follows. To begin with, there was that essential choir for the chapter. This was divided off from the nave by a large stone screen, on the western side of which there was an altar—the nave altar. Eastward of the choir there was a wide space called the presbytery, then the high altar. Thus the church was virtually a double church with the upper end specially appropriated to the college of canons (the chapter) or the monastic body, while the nave had its altar for use of the laity.

The ordinary parish church was often a building of one stage only—one range of ground-floor windows and then the roof. Many, however, especially those built or rebuilt in the fifteenth century, were in two stages, having an upper row of lights—the *clerestory*. Cathedrals and all the greater collegiate churches were given, in addition, a *triforium* gallery—midway between the nave arcade and the clerestory. This served no practical or ceremonial purpose but, carried round the choir as well as the nave, it added considerably to the dignified appearance of the church. In France, it was thought essential for a cathedral to have three towers, central tower and two at the west end to balance an imposing façade. In England the three-tower rule was by no means regularly observed; but its effect (with and without spires) is well seen in the pictures of Durham and Lichfield on pages 69, 77. One of the particular charms of our cathedrals is that they are much more varied and individual in plan and design than the great churches of the Continent.

Another distinctive feature of the old cathedrals was the number of side-chapels added to the main structure. The Normans invariably built a rounded apse at the east end with chapels radiating from it, an arrangement still preserved at Norwich. Chapels were also projected from the eastern wall of the transepts. But the English had a strong predeliction for a square east end and, when rebuilding the choir, always substituted this form for the apse. In the thirteenth century, when the cult of the Virgin became popular, a large Lady Chapel, often the size of a parish church, was added beyond the east wall. This use had already come in when Salisbury Cathedral was begun in 1220 so that the architect was able to incorporate the Lady Chapel as an integral part of his fine design.

The great monastic church of the Benedictine Order had all the appointments of a cathedral except a bishop's seat; for the abbot, though he professed the utmost Christian humility and signed himself "the servant of the servants of God", was a great personage and often as influential as a bishop, a paradox easily accepted in the Middle Ages, when outward forms of grandeur were inseparable from the idea of the majesty of God in the minds of most men, though what was done "to the glory of God" was quite naturally mixed with some local and personal pride in the achievement.

The Cistercian movement of the eleventh century was a sudden and surprisingly vehement revolt against this attitude of mind. It rejected all superfluities in the observance of the monastic ideal beyond what was laid down by St. Benedict in the sixth century. The most rigorous Puritan of Cromwellian times was hardly more ascetic in his views of the simple religious life or so sweeping in his condemnation of distracting ornament than the stern pioneer of the movement, the Englishman, Stephen Harding. But, unlike the Puritans, his followers had no thought of breaking out of the pale of the Church, or attempting to lay down a new rule in place of that given by St. Benedict. They were, in the strictest sense of the word, conformists. The whole burden of their complaint against the old and long established Benedictine communities was that, in observance, they had grown stale and slack, and that the simple message of the Gospel had been dissipated in a round of ceremonial and an excess of worldly concern with great buildings and altars richly dight.

Therefore they would seek to build away from the settlements of men in wild and untamed country. Their clothing would be of undyed sheeps' wool, their church vestments of plain and cheap materials; on their altars no gold or silver furnishings but a wooden crucifix and candlesticks of iron. In their church building not only was carved work banned but the triforium gallery ruled out as an inessential vanity. Nor must there be any high towers, and only one bell to announce the hour of services. Their first experiment was in the midmost thicket of a Burgundian forest where they hewed themselves a wooden monastery and named it Citeaux (Latinised into *Cistercium*). This took place in 1098. Just thirty years later, the first colony came to England and settled at Waverley. In 1132 another colony went to the wild country of the Cleveland Hills in Yorkshire and settled in the valley of the little river Rie, from which they named their house Rievaulx (p. 79). This became one of the most famous of all the Cistercian monasteries and the mother of a number of outstanding houses including Melrose.

The movement was a tremendous success, both in France and England. These monks who went out "into the wilderness" were determined to convert their domains into fruitful lands. They had a strong and up-to-date agricultural policy and gave shelter, a livelihood, and God's blessing to a host of lay brothers who cleared and tilled the land. They became breeders of stock, and eventually sheep-farmers on a large scale. Today it is the beauty of the situation which strikes us most when coming on a ruin of one of their abbeys, not the barren or unkempt wildness of the scene.

Our principal heirlooms in buildings from the days of the monasteries are those bequeathed by the Benedictines and the Cistercians. The former have left us great churches, virtually intact, for they were a town-dwelling community and it was found useful at the Reformation to convert their churches either to cathedral or parish use. Chester, Gloucester, and Peterborough were made the centres of new dioceses and the churches of their great abbeys, which in all respects were ready-made cathedrals, were now confirmed in that rank. At the same time, the churches of the Augustinian Canons at Oxford and Bristol were also made the seats of new bishoprics. Two of the greater Benedictine abbeys, St. Albans and Tewkesbury (p. 51) had their churches saved through the townsmen buying them from the King for parochial use. The former has, in recent times been made a cathedral.

No such salvation came to the churches of the Cistercian abbeys which lay in the depths of the country, in those wildernesses which they had made blossom, but carefully preserved from any tendency to populate. They with their cloisters and domestic buildings fell into picturesque ruin to which processes of preservation have been applied in our own time. As ruins, they are the most picturesque of any, a thing which would greatly have shocked the original authors of the Order. For what makes them such particular objects of beauty is just what was not intended, that is, their gradual decline from the strict austerity rule which governed all Cistercian buildings in the first burst of reforming enthusiasm. At Fountains and Buildwas the twelfth-century naves still retain their walls and arcades and we can see that the triforium gallery has been obediently omitted, to the obvious impoverishment of the appearance of these two great churches.

By the thirteenth century evasions had crept in. In the rebuilt choir of Rievaulx, carried out in the Early English style, the triforium is back in place, giving that height and a sense of grandeur to the building which is its aesthetic function. That is just a plain breach of the law. But in the matter of carvings, here is an evasion which has been subtly turned to better advantage than the thing evaded. Capitals and brackets are *moulded* instead of being *carved* with the usual conventional foliage of the period. This has imposed restraint on the designer of those plain rounds and hollows who has used his medium to the very best advantage, giving the choir a harmonious unity that could not have been achieved by "carving". Empty and roofless as it is, this choir remains one of the most inspiring of our religious buildings. Another, and for the same reasons, is the Chapel of the Nine Altars at Fountains. But the architectural story at Fountains is carried into the fifteenth century when all restraint has disappeared and a great bell-tower, four stages high, proclaims the power and pride of Abbot Huby by having his personal coat of arms and initials boldly carved on its eastern face. Yet we must surely be thankful for that perfect *ensemble* of ruin and setting which is the Fountains we have inherited, however it came about.

VII The Religious House

THE religious (to use that curious noun which looks like an adjective) were of three kinds (if we exclude the hermits). They were monks, who had so far abjured the world that they seldom ventured into it beyond their convent walls except on some official errand; canons, who lived under a rule in their monasteries but regularly attended to the spiritual needs of the laity in their neighbourhood; lastly, the friars, who spent the greater part of their time in the outer world carrying out their special mission of preaching everywhere and, to a limited extent, teaching in the universities.

The houses of the monks (with the single exception of the Carthusians) and of the canons were so identical in plan that if only a single part of one of them still remains standing above ground the remainder can generally be inferred from it. This monastery was built round a covered alley called the cloister, of which the principal building, the church, formed one side (the south being preferred as sunnier than the north, though the nature of the site did not always make this possible, as at Canterbury, Durham, Chester, and Gloucester). Adjoining the transept of the church was the chapter-house and dormitory forming the eastern range; then, on the side opposite to the church, the refectory. The fourth side was occupied by the cellarer who superintended the catering of the establishment. The guest-house was sometimes combined with his quarters in this western range.

The Cistercian plan differed slightly from the Benedictine, because of the large community of lay-brothers which formed a part of the establishment of this Order. They were accommodated in a greatly enlarged western range where they had their own dormitory and refectory. To make extra room, the Cistercians built the refectory of the monks at right angles to the cloister, instead of parallel to it, as in the case of the Benedictines. The Carthusians, who led a partly hermit life and ate and slept in separate cells, lived in a much larger cloister with their cells and gardens ranged round it—as can still be seen at Mount Grace, near Osmotherley in Yorkshire. That uniform plan of the other Orders remained with only slight variations, such as an additional cloister for the infirmary and separate buildings for abbot's and prior's lodgings, from the Norman Conquest to the dissolution in the sixteenth century. But it appears to have been a plan that was not fixed and consolidated until the eleventh century. It had in common with other domestic establishments of the manor-house and castle one feature, the great hall (the refectory), though in the monastery this was not used either as a general day-room—for the monks studied and worked in the cloister—or as a dormitory, for which separate provision was made. But it was given a dais for the high table where the upper members of the community sat. An additional fitting, not found in other halls, was a stone pulpit built into and projecting from one wall from which a reader edified the brethren at meat.

It seems likely that the cloister plan influenced design in both the house and the castle, producing the courtyard type of the fourteenth century, and it seems fairly obvious that the colleges of the old Universities were a direct copy of the monastic cloister. The only difference is that the hall and college chapel are not normally on opposite sides of the quadrangle but in the contiguous ones; that was to suit the master of the college whose needs were different from those of the head of a monastery.

The colleges of Oxford and Cambridge represent the last uninterrupted living link with the claustral life and its buildings. Their Fellows and scholars share with the barristers of the Inns of Court the interesting distinction of being the last traditional users of the great hall, with its dais and high table, where men are still graded into upper and lower classes, though the distinction is purely academic and not social.

VIII The Countryside

THE last half-century has probably seen more really profound alterations in the English countryside than any single generation has known. In the earlier days there might be some great national upset like the Norman Conquest which would make things seem very different for a while, but there would be a gradual sliding back into old ways. Former upheavals were man-made and reversible; today it is the machine which has changed ways and ideas, and from this mastery there can be no going back.

At the beginning of the century, except on the railways and in the factories, the horse was still the prime-mover. He set the pace for ploughing, going to market, and social intercourse. And this pace allowed men to "take their time" and to "do things thoroughly". The market-towns, the villages, and the open country preserved ways and traditions that were of long standing and had their roots deep down in history. And it happened, too, that everything was in better fettle, more serene and prosperous than ever before, a state of affairs that was indeed largely due to the first stage of mechanical development. After the first pains of the Industrial Revolution the machines had made England the first commercial power in the world. That had left an ugly mark in the great towns, but quite the reverse in the countryside. Those machines were steam-driven and their sphere of influence strictly limited.

It is the second phase, in which the internal combustion engine was developed, which has made the great and unreversible break with the past. But the alterations have been all on the material side. Speed used to be a marvel and the Flying Scotsman regarded as the personification of speed because it could arrive in Edinburgh within eight hours of leaving London. Now we can get to New York quicker than that and speed has lost its prestige. What is admired now is peace and quietness. This is still to be found in the countryside where, in spite of speeding the plough with petroleum, man cannot move faster than the seasons. The true English countryman adapts himself to changed circumstances, but his heart and his prejudices are little affected. In general, this spirit pervades the whole of his realm. Village and market-town have adapted themselves to the new age without any revolutionary clean-sweep and have managed to retain that mysterious and refreshing quality of being countrified.

In villages there are still "greens" which, from various origins (often forgotten), have acquired a prescriptive right not to be built on, where village cricket is still played with all the serious excitement of yesteryear. Where there are no longer teamsters to lead the horse to the water and no more witches to duck, the horse-pond is often left undisturbed, to the great profit of waterfowl and artists.

The market-town, on market-day, with its new shop-fronts and motor-borne visitors in tourist-motley has a certain gaiety which it used not to possess. But the excessive bucolic liveliness which formerly transfigured it once a week on this particular day and for a whole week at fair-time vanished in one year or another between the two wars. For the new form of transportation enabled an enterprising auctioneer to set up a "mart" on the outskirts of the town instead of the old beast-market in the market-square, a space provided for this purpose in times out of mind, before the compilation of Domesday Book. It was the forum of the countryside, where news and views circulated, while the wits of farmer v. farmer and farmer v. dealer were pitted sharply against each other and bargains made by the morally uplifting process of "handfast" with spiritous reinforcement at the inn. From voices raised above the babel of the beasts, one caught snatches of the drollest and most trenchant repartee, enriched by the still undiluted dialect of the particular region. On the arcaded floor of the market-house, men stood by open sacks of their own grain (from which the market official had scooped out the toll due to the lord of the manor). And there, or on the steps of the market-cross, if there was one, sat the farmers' wives with ample baskets of eggs and butter and trussed fowls. Stalls and booths lined the pavements which radiated into the town.

The auction mart is commercially much more efficient than the cluttered up arena of the time-honoured haggling-bout, but for social contacts, and as a school of wit and land-wisdom, it is no substitute. The absence of other diversions proper to market-day in the market-square, down to the end of the eighteenth century, cannot be regretted—the horrible sport of bull-baiting and the public whipping of men and women.

The oldest fixture of the market-square was the high-cross, the steps of which acted as stalls, usually for a privileged few of the townsmen. Occasionally they were roofed-in and given an architectural treatment, of which fine mediaeval examples survive at Salisbury and Chichester. But all were a target for the first reformers and the later Puritans who knocked the heads of the crosses down, if they did no further damage. Other permanent buildings were a guildhall, a moot-hall, and a market-hall. In post-mediaeval times the last pair were usually combined in a two or three storeyed building, of which the market-hall with its small toll-house and lock-up occupied the ground-floor and was open on all sides to the square. The moot-hall, or town court-room, where local justice was dispensed, was placed above that. Sometimes there was a further storey above that again. One such at Thaxted is shown on page 53.

This homely building is the ancestor of the town hall which, within the last century, has become so much larger and more pretentious, and its original compact arrangement of covered market, small prison, law-court, mayor's parlour, town clerk's office and even guildhall (as at Exeter) is now dispersed into a range of "municipal buildings". Several of the old moot-halls remain, constructed variously in stone, brick, and half-timber. The picturesque form of the latter has on more than one occasion saved it from being swept away—the fate of most of them.

The half-timbered building had several advantages over the more rigid construction. It was primarily a carpenter's and not a mason's or brick-layer's job, and could be made complete for assembly in the carpenter's yard. When erected over a site of limited size it could enlarge itself in the upper storeys by a projecting overhang—a facility that was usually taken advantage of, as seen in the pictures on pages 51, 53, 91, 93. Finally, it could, if necessary, be taken to pieces and moved to another site, without undue difficulty, even if it had been standing in the same place for two or three hundred years. Moving house (thus literally) has been quite a general practice in Shrewsbury where more than one old black-and-white beauty, which has all the appearance of having grown on the spot to which it is now rooted, was really designed for a frontage in quite a different street—usually when Charles II was king.

Another regular feature of one side of the market-square is the principal tavern of the town, which now usually signs itself "Hotel", a word never heard of in the market-town or village before the nineteenth century. This *inn*, to give it its most proper and general title, has been one of the three essential buildings in nearly every place—the others being the church and the manor-house. The inn was intimately concerned with the welfare of the life of the community in more ways than one. Perhaps its most important function was to give rest and shelter to man and beast of the pack-horse train which was the commercial link of the remote settlement with the seaport town and old centres of production of cloth and linen piece-goods. Much of these imports would be destined for sale in the market-square, on which the inn looked out, and much could be inspected in the large yard behind it, where packmen and pedlars would often display their wares, as in an open-air showroom.

Another function of this useful public house was to provide the farmers who foregathered on market-day with a cheap and filling dinner called the "farmers' ordinary". For this, a special long room of the hall-type, projecting into the ample yard from the back of the inn, was usually provided. The farmers' ordinary is not quite extinct but, where found, it has usually been relegated to one of the lesser hostelries. The trade of the principal inn was further reinforced when turnpike trusts improved the roads and stage-coaches became more numerous and, further, by the introduction of the mail-coach in the late eighteenth century and the increased popularity of posting by chaise. This trade was killed suddenly in the middle decades of the last century by the railways. But there has been a great revival with the coming of the motorist. And for this act of preservation of an essential countryside feature we have, indeed, to thank the internal combustion engine; for many a fine old hostelry, now cherished and often carefully restored, would certainly have mouldered away but for the timely intervention of this otherwise doubtful blessing.

Index

The numerals in **bold** type denote the page numbers of the illustrations

HOUSES AND PALACES

MONASTERIES

TOWN AND COUNTRY

Hadrian's Wall, at Cuddy's Crag, near Housesteads, Northumberland

The great Wall of Hadrian was built in the early second century across the lower neck of Britain, between the estuaries of Tyne and Solway, a distance of seventy-three miles. Its parapet-walk is judged to have stood about twenty feet high and it was embattled throughout at intervals of a mile with a strong point (mile-castle) which could be garrisoned by fifty men. At lesser intervals between these mile-castles were two turrets and, immediately within the shelter of the wall, sixteen full-sized forts, for permanent garrisons were disposed along its length. The most impressive sector at the present day is (as shown) where the Wall follows the precipitous intrusion of basaltic rock—the Whin Sill—commanding long views over the wild fell country of old Caledonia. When first built, it was the intention of the Roman government to complete the conquest of the whole of Caledonia which had been almost secured by Agricola in the first century, and another wall of turf was made by Hadrian's successor, Antoninus Pius, across the Forth-Clyde isthmus, with advance posts established still further north. All these forward positions had to be abandoned, however, and Hadrian's Wall, several times repaired and restored, remained the boundary of the Roman Empire in the north-west until the general collapse in the fifth century. Its ruin in a still wild countryside never fails to stir the imagination of anyone who follows the line of that ancient and fateful frontier.

The Tower of London

The Tower of London was built by William the Conqueror twelve years after the Battle of Hastings. He placed it just within the old Roman wall in the angle made by its junction with the river to impress the citizens with his military power and the completeness of his conquest. Only for a short interval in the twelfth century did the City gain authority over it—its eighteen acres still form a separate liberty within the City boundary. In the thirteenth and fourteenth centuries the old plan of adjacent wards was improved by two successive rings of curtain wall with flanking towers at intervals converting it into that of a concentric castle. The Tower has played the part of fortress, palace, and state prison. It is still garrisoned by a contingent of the regular army and the gate guarded by a small permanent body of yeomen warders who still wear the Tudor dress. They came into being when Henry VIII ceased to use the Tower as a royal residence but wished it to be still considered a palace and left twelve members of the yeomen of the guard to be on permanent station there. The eleventh-century Norman keep (the White Tower—in earlier days it was refreshed with a coat of whitewash each year) appears in the middle of the picture and one of the towers of the inner curtain—the Lanthorn Tower—immediately in front of it, while St. Thomas's Tower, which covers the old approach by water—the Traitors' Gate—is on the left. In the distance is seen the monument surmounting the Port of London Authority offices. It stands on Tower Hill overlooking the site of the scaffold where so many historical notables faced the block.

Westminster Abbey, London

This picture shows the west front of the Abbey church and, to the right, the Victoria Tower of the Houses of Parliament. The group is an interesting study in Period reproductions. The church of the Benedictine Abbey, first raised by Edward the Confessor in the eleventh century as a Norman building, was then converted by Henry III to one conforming with the new Gothic manner (now called the Early English style). Continuity was halted from time to time in carrying out this transformation down the nave, so that the western façade was not reached until the fifteenth century, when the Perpendicular style had set in (a change but not a break in the life-cycle of the vigorous Gothic tradition). But even then (the distraction provided by Henry VII's chapel intervening) the west front was not completed before the dissolution of the monastery in 1540. The work of adding the upper stages to the two flanking towers and finishing off the gable was never attempted until 1713, when Sir Christopher Wren produced designs to this end. Construction was put in hand, but before it had got very far Wren died and his pupil, Hawksmoor, carried on with modifications of his own. Neither did he survive until completion, which was not reached until 1740. Now we can see and compare at our leisure the genuine Gothic work from the ground up to the solid unmoulded horizontal course bestriding the apex of the great west window. All above that is the Stuart-Georgian finale of Edward the Confessor's undertaking. And it must surely strike one as an attempt by classically-minded architects not so much to reproduce the Gothic original (of which they were confessedly contemptuous), but to show how they firmly believed it *ought* to have been built. The innuendo is as plain as the pinnacles which they sought to improve on by adding to their raw mediaeval austerity the curl of Roman consoles. But the Gothic Revivalists of the nineteenth century were quite the other way inclined. It was their burning and humble desire to recapture the Gothic spirit. And they succeeded in catching a better likeness than the would-be improvers of the Abbey. But still it was a Victorian likeness and not a mediaeval reincarnation. And that likeness was probably never caught more attractively than by Sir Charles Barry in his Victoria Tower.

The Thames at Westminster, London

In the picture the Houses of Parliament appear on the left with the Victoria Tower (340 ft.) in the foreground. At the other end of the group is the clock-tower where the chimes, composed by a Cambridge don in 1792 for the University Church now sounds round the world at 9 p.m. His name is not so well remembered as that of Ben Hall, First Commissioner of Works when the clock-tower was completed. On the river front, the near pair of towers contains the library, the other, the Speaker's residence. Between them lies the Terrace. On the right bank stand St. Thomas's Hospital and the County Hall, parliament-house of the London County Council. Catching the sunlight above Westminster Bridge is the clock-tower of the Shell-Mex building. The group of buildings forming the Houses of Parliament is still called officially the Palace of Westminster and sometimes alluded to as "St. Stephen's", names which have an interesting significance. The original palace was a hall built by King Canute. It was enlarged by Edward the Confessor when he undertook the building of the Abbey, with its great church dedicated to St. Peter, opposite. Subsequent kings enlarged the palace and used it as a convenient place to establish the royal courts of justice. When the institution of Parliament was established in the thirteenth century it gradually became the rule for the Upper House to sit in a chamber of the palace, the Commons sitting in the chapter-house of the Abbey, until the end of Henry VIII's reign, when both Houses sat in the palace. The Palace of Westminster took fire in 1834 and was destroyed, except for the great hall (now called Westminster Hall) and the undercroft of St. Stephen's Chapel, first built by William the Conqueror and dedicated to that saint as a thank-offering for the crown which had been placed on his head on St. Stephen's Day. The present buildings were designed by Sir Charles Barry entirely as a home for the British Parliament, the highest of the royal courts. There was no thought of restoring the palace; but the old name sticks.

London from Waterloo Bridge

A view of the City looking towards Blackfriars Bridge and the Thames Embankment. The dome of St. Paul's Cathedral is conspicuous on the right and, on the left, that of the Central Criminal Court (the Old Bailey) which stands on the site of Newgate Gaol. Just to the left of it is the steeple of St. Bride's Church, Fleet St., built by Wren in 1671. Between these two landmarks and the river, trees mask the buildings of the Middle and Inner Temple, legal societies, constituted like the colleges of a university, which established themselves here in the fourteenth century in buildings belonging to the recently dissolved Order of the Knights Templars. Here too, are the Temple gardens where Shakespeare placed the ominous picking of the red and white roses (Henry IV, Part I, Act II, Sc. 4). Several great houses, including the Savoy Palace, stood beside the river west of the Temple, each with access to the waterway by stairs, of which Essex Stairs is a relic. All memory of the old irregular shore with its exposed mud-banks at low tide was swept away in 1864 with the building of the Thames Embankment. The lighters at moorings in mid-stream are laden with goods in transhipment between vessels lying in the Pool and warehouses on the South Bank.

Buckingham Palace, London

It takes its name from the earlier Buckingham House, built for John Sheffield, Duke of Buckingham and Normanby, in 1702. This was bought by George III as a dower house for his Queen in 1762. It was called the Queen's House but they both resided here (as Fanny Burney's Diary describes), holding courts at St. James's. Queen Charlotte, however, predeceased the King, who died in 1820. His successor, George IV, had a passion for finery of all kinds combined with a dash of the nobler flair of the connoisseur. He had employed John Nash to lay out Regent's Park and build Regent Street and he now set him to transform the House into a really royal palace, regardless of cost. Retaining a mere shell of the earlier building, Nash proceeded on the plan of a large single court, closed on three sides but open towards the east, except for a triumphal arch. The palace was still far from habitable ten years hence, when King George died, to be succeeded by William IV.

Under the new regime Nash's ideas and methods were considered too extravagant. He was replaced by Edward Blore who had just built Abbotsford for Sir Walter Scott. Blore made considerable alterations in Nash's designs and the palace was not ready until May, 1837, too late for King William to enjoy, for he died the next month, but in July the young Queen Victoria moved in.

In 1845 the Queen, now a wife and mother, had to complain that the accommodation was much too limited. Blore, still the presiding architectural genius, remedied this by closing the fourth side of the quadrangle with a range of building facing down the Mall. This meant moving the triumphal arch which was re-erected at the north-east corner of Hyde Park where it is now known as the Marble Arch. Blore's east front was altered again in 1913 to its present appearance (with the now familiar royal balcony) by Sir Aston Webb.

Buckingham Palace has become the regular London home of the Sovereign, though the style "Court of St. James" is still used on royal proclamations. The forecourt of the palace is on the site of the Mulberry Garden planted by James I to promote a home-grown silk industry for England.

Winchester, Hampshire

Winchester is a city which has repeatedly taken a lead in our national history, and more than once played a supreme part in it. The Romans found the powerful Celtic tribe of the Belgae in occupation of the hill from which the picture is taken (their defence works can still be seen) and they set about romanising them by founding a cantonal town in the valley below—*Venta Belgarum*. From thence, they drove roads over the chalk downs, giving access from the west, north, and north-east (all still in use). The Saxons made Winchester the royal capital of Wessex and, as it grew to supreme power above the other kingdoms, it became the principal seat of the king of all England, not being supplanted by London until late in the eleventh century. King Alfred, who ruled from Winchester, was a patron of learning whose influence was long felt, and here, in the fourteenth century, the great bishop, William of Wykeham, devised a complete system of education, and gave it material effect by founding a school for the young at Winchester and a college for those scholars in Oxford—both now in their fifth century of vigorous life. In the great hall of the castle Parliament has several times assembled, and there hangs on one of its walls the top of an enormous round table called "King Arthur's". Antiquaries do not concede it an earlier date than the thirteenth century, but Henry VII, who favoured the Arthurian romance for political reasons, had figures of all the knights painted clockwise round the rim—as can still be seen. In the picture two symbolic monuments of our cultural history are plain—the tower, transepts, and choir of Wykeham's cathedral and, in mid-street on the right, the statue of King Alfred.

Bristol, Gloucestershire

Next to London, Bristol has probably had the most varied and intensive history of any English town. The Normans recognised it as a vital strategic key to the west and gave it a strong castle and protective wall. By the middle of the fourteenth century it had become entitled to call itself a county with shire jurisdiction and, in the seventeenth century, it became an ecclesiastical city. What with a well organised traffic through its seaport and the woollen industry then flourishing both to the north and south-west of it, its merchants became rich and powerful. The picture is taken from the Cabot Tower, a monument erected in 1897 to commemorate the explorers, John Cabot and his sons, of whom the second, Sebastian, was the most notable. In 1496, Henry VII had granted letters patent to John and his sons to search for the new lands in the west and "a passage to Cathay", only four years after the successful voyage of Columbus. The Cabots made their landfall at Nova Scotia (where a similar tower has been erected) and Cape Breton. It was largely through Sebastian's foresight and efforts that the great fraternity of Merchant Adventurers was founded and he became their first governor. The picture shows the view to the north (away from the waterfront). The most prominent feature is the tower of the University, completed in 1925 and opened by King George V, after whom the ten-ton bell in its octagon is named—Great George. The new hall of the Grammar School (founded by Henry VIII in 1532) appears on the left. Bristol's triumphs are now in the high air as well as on the high seas.

Ludlow Castle, Shropshire

Ludlow Castle is here seen from across the River Teme which, with the sharp rise of the ground, forms a natural defence to its western side; the walls which enclosed the town gave it additional protection elsewhere. It was the chief stronghold of the Mortimers, the most powerful of the Lords Marchers, until the last of their line took it to the crown in the person of Edward IV. Shortly afterwards the castle became the headquarters of the Council of Wales and the Marches, as told on page 16. Milton, who was on the staff of the Earl of Bridgewater, Lord President of the Council, wrote the Masque of Comus here, which was first performed in the great hall of the castle in 1634. The inauguration of the Council brought great prosperity to the town, and many fine houses of that time, built for use of the officials of the court, remain, making Ludlow one of the most interesting and picturesque towns of the Welsh Border. Its fine parish church of St. Lawrence, endowed by many rich guilds and still retaining much old glass and woodwork, is seen beyond the castle. The sharp-featured Clee hills rise in the distance.

Tewkesbury, Gloucestershire

The picture shows the old water-mill in the foreground which figures prominently in Mrs. Craik's *John Halifax, Gentleman*. It was working until recent years, taking its power from a branch of Shakespeare's Avon. In the distance appears the Norman tower of the great Benedictine Abbey church where so many historical personages lie, including those who fell in, or were beheaded after, the Battle of Tewkesbury, 1471, which was fatal to the Lancastrian cause and placed the Yorkist claimant, Edward IV, firmly on the throne. When the Abbey was dissolved in 1539 the townsmen purchased the church for £435. It has since been their parish church and has been well preserved, with its monuments and some fine stained glass of the fourteenth century. The picture is taken from the Ham, a huge town meadow, 200 acres in extent, round which the Severn flows and joins its tidal waters at its last weir, fitted with lock gates to make the river navigable, also the Avon, whose main branch enters at this point. The bore-wave which runs up the Severn at each high tide reaches the foot of this weir. In the town there is much half-timber work in the old inns and houses.

The Moot-hall, Thaxted, Essex

This is an excellent example both of half-timbered construction and of the type of public building set up in the sixteenth and seventeenth centuries from which our town-halls are descended. Standing in the market-square, it provides on its ground-floor a covered market for grain and other commodities likely to be damaged by the weather. On the first floor is (or was) the court-room, where the justices sat, whose dooms could often be expeditiously carried out at the stocks or the whipping-post, located in the square or by the church gate. It was unusual to have a second floor, as seen here, but that could be put to several uses from the purposes of a guildhall to a wool-store—and there used to be an important wool market at Thaxted. The town was formerly an incorporated borough, but lost its charter in the time of James II. While half-timbered buildings in the western shires were designed to show their wooden ribs, in East Anglia these were usually concealed under plaster, often decorated with pargetting, a sensible precaution which no doubt kept the house warmer. In the present instance, however, posts and curved braces were evidently meant to be seen and admired, as the first-floor windows are disposed in a neat Gothic arcade. As mentioned in the text (p. 28), one of the advantages of this construction was that you could increase your floor-space at the rise of every storey. This was contrived by running diagonal beams (dragon-beams) through the floor-joists and out to the corners, where they were supported (as seen) by brackets which often received the attention of the carver. Thaxted has an exceedingly fine church with the only mediaeval stone spire in the county. It is just seen in the background with the typical East Anglian feature of light flying buttress thrown between pinnacle and spire.

Henley-on-Thames, Oxfordshire

Henley is best known for its regatta which takes place early in July in the straight mile of the river, which begins just beyond the bridge. This aquatic festival was inaugurated in 1839, just ten years after Cambridge first challenged Oxford "to row a match at or near London, each in an eight-oared boat during the ensueing Easter Vacation"; a gage which Oxford accepted and won the first of the famous series. Henley Week is now taken for granted as supplementary to the other. The bridge was designed by William Hayward who had been assistant to John Gwynne (a fellow Salopian) when building Magdalen Bridge, Oxford (illustrated on page 103). It was completed in 1786 after Hayward had died and been laid in the parish church. The carvings of Father Thames and the maid Isis, which decorate the keystones of the central arch, were the work of one of our earlier sculptresses, Mrs. Damer, a native genius, the daughter of Field-Marshal Conway of Park Place (up on the left bank). They are an interesting memento for, apart from her doings as an artist, she was notable for her wide social contacts, having named among her friends Nelson and Napoleon. When the latter was in retirement at St. Helena she sent him her bust of Charles James Fox, whom her father had supported in politics. Her cousin, Horace Walpole, made her his residuary legatee and left her a life interest in Strawberry Hill.

ENTERPRISE
JACKO

Dover Castle, Kent

Dover Castle has been called "the key to England". From its battlements the coast of France can be plainly seen on any average clear day. Its keep and inner ward (with square towers) were made in the latter days of Henry II. The former rises on walls 24 feet thick. Just to the left of it is seen the forebuilding protecting the entrance to the keep which is at first-floor level. Gardrobes are located in the central projection between the corner towers—in matters of sanitary convenience the Normans were much ahead of the builders of great mansions in the seventeenth and eighteenth century. The outer curtain, a work of the late thirteenth century, shows the improved flanking-tower which is round instead of square. Its battlements were shorn off at a much later period, in connection with defence works undertaken when an invasion by Napoleon Bonaparte was looked for, to which time belongs the ravelin in the foreground. On the right is the Constable's Gate, the main entrance to the castle, and one of the most imposing and picturesque of any of our castle gatehouses.

Windsor Castle, Berkshire

This great palace-fortress is the same age as the Tower of London (eleventh century), but the Tower has not been used as a royal residence since the time of Henry VIII. Windsor (which has fewer grim memories, though state prisoners have often been lodged there) has always been the favourite and most frequented of the royal residences. One of its chief attractions from the very beginning was its game preserve in the Great Park and Windsor Forest which William the Conqueror acquired from the monks of Westminster in exchange for two Essex manors. The picture, taken from the left bank of the Thames, shows the western aspect of the castle, with St. George's Chapel (where the knights of the garter are installed) on the right. In the middle stands the round keep, a work begun by the Conqueror and completed up to the point where the buttresses can be seen to fade out by Henry II. Above that, with battlements and turret, is an addition made by George IV in the early nineteenth century. On the left are the state apartments, overlooking the North Terrace, a huge reconstruction of the same time. A note on the castle is on page 17.

Bodiam Castle, Sussex

Bodiam Castle combines the salient features of military fortress architecture as developed during the thirteenth century with the improved plan of the single rectangular courtyard surrounded by continuous ranges of permanent buildings which had evolved by the middle of the fourteenth century. It was built in 1385 by an old soldier who had served in France under Edward III, primarily as a private residence but capable of strong resistance in case of a foreign invasion of the south coast. It was made the centre of an artificial lake instead of a moat which, to all appearances would seem more effective, though it might have been more easily drained by a determined enemy. The entrance (over a modern causeway) is on the far side of the castle to that appearing in the picture, which shows the postern gate in the middle tower whose projecting battlements defend it with a strong and picturesque array of *machicoulis*. Though the interior has been dismantled the walls have not been damaged by war or the official demolitions of the Commonwealth Government. It is one of our most romantic-looking ruins, especially when the white water-lily is in flower on the bosom of the lake.

St. Michael's Mount, Cornwall

This island, whose name and appearance strike such a romantic note, fulfils all expectation in its strange history. The clustered buildings on the summit comprise a former priory of the Benedictine Order, a castle, and a lordly residence. As a monastery, its story probably goes back to the legendary days of the Celtic Church. But its first appearance on record is in the eleventh century, when Edward the Confessor presented the island to its larger counterpart in shape and name across the Channel, in the Norman Bay of Avranches—the island monastery of Mont St. Michel. As a castle, it has had a more exciting history than many of the larger ones. The sea, which is an open road to all continents, is a poor substitute for the ordinary moat. This and its detachment, except at low tide, made it a tempting prize for a marauding rebel, and three notable ones managed to seize and hold it, two of them with creditable success, against heavy odds. They were Henry de Pomeroy, a backer of Prince John, when he tried to seize power during his brother's (King Richard I's) imprisonment on the Continent; John de Vere, Earl of Oxford, a determined Lancastrian who arrived from France with two ships in 1473 and held it against the Sheriff and all the king's men after the cause of the red rose was believed to be lost; and the infamous Perkin Warbeck, who gained temporary possession in 1497. During the Civil War, a royalist garrison held out there stoutly and successfully until King Charles's cause was irretrievably lost elsewhere. In 1660 it was acquired by the St. Aubyn family, who lived there keeping the old monastic refectory in use as a dining-hall. The Mount remained in that family until, in 1953, its head, the 3rd Lord St. Levan, presented it to the National Trust.

H.M.S. *Victory*, Portsmouth Dockyard, Hampshire

The long and splendid era of sail has passed away with only two attempts made to preserve for posterity actual ships of the winds. It is something to be thankful for that the experiment has been tried and that each chosen vessel was an outstanding member of her class, in design, accomplishment, and sentiment. These heirlooms are the tea-clipper, *Cutty Sark*, and H.M.S. *Victory*. Each has not only been saved from destruction but restored to the fine figure she once made. The *Victory* already had honours enough to commend her for preservation before the episode of Trafalgar. Laid down in 1758, launched in 1765, she was flagship successively to Admirals Hardy, Geary, Hyde Parker, Kempenfelt, Howe, Hood and Jervis. Wearing the flag of the latter she, with only thirteen of her sisters, destroyed the Spanish fleet of twenty-seven line-of-battle ships off Cape St. Vincent in 1797, Nelson, in the *Captain*, taking a leading part of the action (though breaking the rules to do it). After forty-six years of service the *Victory* was laid up for two years undergoing a complete refit. She was commissioned again in 1803 as the flagship of Lord Nelson, commander-in-chief of the British fleet. In the action at Trafalgar she was so badly damaged that she had to be towed into Gibraltar where jury masts were rigged under which she sailed for home with Nelson's body on board, taking 49 days to reach the Thames. In her latter days she remained afloat in Portsmouth Harbour, still in commission as the flagship of the Portsmouth Command. In 1922 funds were raised by public subscription to restore her, complete with masts, rigging, sails, and gear as she appeared on the first Trafalgar Day.

Canterbury Cathedral, Kent

The official date given for the foundation of the cathedral is 597, the year when St. Augustine with his mission from Rome to the Saxons landed in Kent. But Bede, who lived only a hundred years later, records that Augustine restored the ruin of a church "which he had been informed had been built by the ancient Roman Christians", which would take the foundation back perhaps three centuries at least to the days of the British (that is, Celtic) Church. Augustine introduced the system of the cathedral-priory, peculiar to England, and a great Benedictine abbey grew up with the church. In 1011 the cathedral was ravaged by the Danes and, though restored by Canute, it was gutted by fire in 1067, and derelict when the first Norman archbishop, Lanfranc, was appointed. Lanfranc pulled the old building down and raised an entirely new one. He would probably have done that, even if the earlier church had not been damaged, as the Normans did not leave a single Saxon cathedral or abbey unreplaced by a building after their own particular design and grandiose ideas. The choir of Lanfranc's cathedral was, in turn, pulled down early in the twelfth century to make room for a still larger one. This, called after the energetic prior, Conrad's Choir, was in existence at the time of the murder of Archbishop Becket, but it was destroyed by fire in 1174. To replace Conrad's Choir, and erect in the new building a shrine to the late Archbishop, who had been martyred only four years before, a supreme effort was made, not merely to repair the damage but to create a worthy and memorable addition. The result was a considerable prolongation of the east end with the famous Trinity Chapel, its crypt, and the further apsidal projection called the Corona. The picture shows the south-east aspect of the cathedral, with the central tower, called Bell Harry (Perpendicular, late fifteenth century) rising above the south-east transept, in the angle of which appears Anselm's Chapel, with its fine window in the Decorated style inserted in 1336. Then follows the Transitional Norman work of the Trinity Chapel and Corona. The monastic buildings occupied the north side of the cathedral.

Durham Cathedral

Durham Cathedral was, until 1836, the seat of a prince-bishop with sovereign powers of jurisdiction, in whose diocese the king's writ did not run. Before the Reformation it had been a cathedral-priory and its choir contained the richest and most deeply venerated shrine in the north of England. Below it lay the relics of St. Cuthbert, Bishop of Lindisfarne in the seventh century, whose body, removed from that island in the earlier Viking raids, was carried from place to place to escape their fury for the space of a hundred and twenty years till it found secure repose on this high rock which rises abruptly in a loop of the River Wear. Over the body of the saint a new cathedral was founded in the year 999.

After the Conquest, a Norman bishop was installed who began rebuilding the cathedral on a very grand scale, attaching to it a Benedictine monastery, building himself a castle-palace and fortifying the whole enclosure of the rock. His successor, the notorious Ralph Flambard, continued the work, which still constitutes the greater part of the building and is our noblest example of Norman manner.

This picture shows the west front of the cathedral with its two towers (Norman in their lower stages). The great west window is an insertion of the fourteenth century. Below it is seen the Lady Chapel, a lovely building in transitional Norman. Its position at the west instead of the east of the great church is unique—and thereby hangs more than one tale. Abutting on the south-west tower is the western range of the monastic cloister with the windows of the monks' dormitory, now used as a library and museum. The central tower is a work of the fifteenth century.

Norwich Cathedral, Norfolk

The cathedral, to which was attached a priory of Benedictine monks, was begun in 1096 with the building of the choir. It is the only one which retains the original Norman plan of rounded apse with projecting chapels. In it the stone seat for the bishop placed there by the founder also survives. The picture shows the south side of the cathedral, with Norman work in transept and tower. The stone spire was built in the middle of the fifteenth century and the battlements added at the same time. This spire had two wooden predecessors. The first was blown down during a gale of 1362 and went through the roof of the choir, damaging the Norman clerestory which was rebuilt immediately afterwards and given larger windows with traceried lights in the prevailing Decorated style (as seen to the right of the picture). In 1463 the second spire was struck by lightning, again damaging the choir roof and setting the old Norman wooden roof of the nave on fire. This accident was much to our present advantage as both roofs were replaced with a splendid stone lierne vault set with a series of boldly carved bosses illustrating Bible stories. The Priory was dissolved in 1538. The sixty-two stalls of the monastic chapter with their carved misericordes are still there, and the two great gateways to the monastic precinct remain quite intact.

Salisbury Cathedral, Wiltshire

Salisbury is of exceptional interest for two reasons. The entire city was founded all at one time—the thirteenth century—and built on a well-contrived grid plan. In the second place, the cathedral is the only ancient one which has come down to us unaltered, so that the plan and architectural style of its original designer remains intact.

What gave rise to this large and comprehensive enterprise at a single date was the resolve of one man, Bishop Richard le Poor, to put an end to the humiliating conditions under which the clergy of the earlier cathedral had to live. They and their church were cooped up within the walls of the fortified hill of Old Sarum (two miles from the present city), a cramped site with access and egress only by grace of the military commander. The Bishop had to chose a site for the great removal that was marshy and liable to flooding, but the scheme was boldly put in hand in the year 1219, and the foundation-stone of the present cathedral laid the following year. The building was completed with a low tower before the end of the century—a complete work in the purest phase of the Early English style. The upper part of the tower with its spire (achieving 404 feet, the highest in England) was added in the fourteenth century, when the Decorated style had come in. This harmonious and masterly conception, rising above the water-meadows and willowy banks of the Avon, drew out the genius of Constable and Turner and, since their day, it has probably been the most sketched, painted, and photographed of any cathedral. Mr. Kersting has chosen a view of the south side within the Close, showing the main and south transepts with a glimpse of the Bishop's Palace.

The Cathedral Close (walled in the fourteenth century with the stones of the abandoned church at Old Sarum) with its mediaeval and Georgian buildings is perhaps the most beautiful enclosure of its kind. The city still keeps its original street plan, retains many old houses and the covered-in market-cross built by a fourteenth-century bishop.

Wells Cathedral, Somerset

The city of Wells is remarkable not only for the chaste beauty of its cathedral but for the number of ancient buildings associated with it that remain well preserved. The most striking is the fortified bishop's palace, with its embattled walls, great gatehouse, and moat (supplied with the copious overflow of St. Andrew's Well, from which the place takes its name). By these sacred springs a church has been founded as early as the seventh century, when Saxon immigrants, the Somersaetas, had penetrated thus far. Two centuries later, when the tribe had settled into fixed boundaries, their shire of Somerset was made a self-contained diocese (which it has remained). But the first Norman bishop chose to move his seat from Wells to the (even then) more fashionable hot springs of Bath, where he built an enormous new church with Benedictine priory attached. A successor, however, returned to Wells within the century. In 1174 the present church was begun in the very latest style, now called Early English. The choir is, in fact, the earliest example in the whole country of that style. Working westwards steadily and without a break, through transept, down nave, the west front was reached in the first decade of the thirteenth century. Then, still without a break, the most distinguished façade of all our great churches was produced with its tier upon tier of statuary, the work occupying perhaps thirty years—to the verge of the period when the Decorated style set in. This uniformity in design and treatment makes Wells comparable only with Salisbury. But at Salisbury there is only a single addition to the main fabric, the upper part of the tower and spire, while at Wells, in the fourteenth century, there was a reconstruction of choir and retrochoir, a Lady Chapel added, and the three towers at successive dates, the third being built in the fifteenth century. The picture shows the south-east aspect of the cathedral with the Early English transept and the central tower and reconstructed east end in the succeeding style, harmonising wonderfully with the earlier work and adding a generous touch of richness (typically Somersaetan) to its more austere forms.

Lichfield Cathedral, Staffordshire

Lichfield is in the heart of the old Saxon kingdom of Mercia to whose boundaries the diocese once extended. It was so large that the bishop required a second cathedral (at first in Chester, later, Coventry). It was St. Chad, Bishop of the Mercians, who, in about the year 670, fixed on Lichfield as the site of his cathedral and the church is dedicated to him. There is nothing left of the Saxon cathedral and very few traces of its Norman successor which was gradually pulled down and replaced by the present purely Gothic building. This work appears to have begun in the first quarter of the thirteenth century and continued into the early part of the fourteenth, with the result that part of the choir is in the Early English style and all else Early Decorated, including the uniquely fine Lady Chapel.

The cathedral approximates more nearly to the Continental model than most, in having three steeples, for long known locally as the "Three Ladies of the Vale" (of Trent), which is not inapt, for the cathedral, small in size, well proportioned, and "dressy" in appearance, suggests the feminine gender in the same way that the Ionic order did to the ancient Greeks. In the Civil War the central spire was completely wrecked by the artillery of the Parliamentary forces which laid siege to the cathedral close. It was restored, together with other much damaged parts, under the energetic direction of Bishop Hackett (appointed 1661) and is a remarkable piece of Gothic restoration undertaken at so late a date. Unhappily, the name of the master-builder who undertook the work is lost. By another piece of good luck the Lady Chapel has regained sufficient old stained glass (sixteenth century) to fill seven of its windows. This was discovered in Belgium in 1802 by, Sir Brooke Boothby, a member of the Lichfield Literary Circle, and bought for £200. It came from the dissolved Convent of Herkenrode*. The picture is taken from the south-west with the Minster Pool in the foreground.

* The remainder of the Herkenrode glass is in St. Mary's Church, Shrewsbury.

Rievaulx Abbey, Yorkshire

This was one of the earliest Cistercian foundations in England (the year 1132) and became one of the most famous and the most active in begetting daughter houses. Situated in the delightful valley of the little River Rie (from which it takes its name), the description of its detachment and setting, written by the monk, Walter Daniel, in the middle of the twelfth century, tallies exactly with what one feels about it today. Now, as seven hundred years ago, the stream "gives out a gentle murmur of soft sound" and "the branches of lovely trees rustle and sing together" so that "the happy listner is filled with a glad jubilee of harmonious sound" and "his ears drink in the feast prepared for them and are satisfied." The nave of the abbey church has almost disappeared, but the choir and transepts, as rebuilt in the thirteenth century, stand to their full height, though, as seen in the picture, all the roofs and the outer walls of the choir are gone; but the openings of the main arcade, triforium, and clerestory, with their mouldings and other restrained ornament are wonderfully preserved. The abbey church is one of the rare instances of deliberate mis-orientation. Dictated by the site, a natural platform on the hillside, the axis of the church has been laid north and south, so that looking towards the high altar one faces south instead of east. The buildings are now under the guardianship of the Ministry of Works. A note on Rievaulx and the Cistercians is on page 23.

Northleach, Gloucestershire

In the mid-fifteenth century, when the wool trade flourished in the Cotswold Hills, Northleach and Chipping Campden were the two pre-eminent rivals as market centres. The latter, being more substantially built in stone, has survived to the present time with much to recall the days of its prosperity and can still be called a *town*, whereas Northleach has shrunk to the size of a small village, with nothing left to suggest a large and busy population except its great church and the records of its manorial court, at which the bailiff dispensed summary justice as deputy for the Abbot of Gloucester who was lord of the manor. The parish church SS. Peter and Paul, which is one of the finest in England, was rebuilt in the earlier part of the fifteenth century, as was that of Chipping Campden. Both have several features which are recognisably identical, including the uncommon octagonal column with hollowed faces, and the masons' marks show that the same craftsmen worked on both restorations. Northleach church is the more attractive building, with architectural graces superior to its rival, and has had the good fortune to preserve the original mediaeval figures in the niches of its superb south porch. In the floor of its nave are the brasses of many of its former woolmen magnates ranging over a span of years from 1400 (when the earlier church stood) to 1525.

Fairford, Gloucestershire

Fairford, though a small and very countrified place between the Cotswold Hills and the Thames Valley, has a far-flung reputation for two things of first quality. One is its trout-fishing in the River Colne which for long has been well looked after and kept stocked, though always available by day-ticket; the other is its parish church. The church is well known because it is the only one in England which has preserved its pre-Reformation glass in every one of its twenty-eight windows almost intact, a fact so striking that it has probably obscured other interesting virtues of this church. It was built in the very last years of the fifteenth century by a rich woolstapler and cloth factor of Cirencester, and represents the very last word in planning and design in the Gothic manner, with the only limitation of fitting an old tower into a new model. The earlier church, pulled down in 1491 to make room for the new, was a cruciform building—an old-fashioned style that had given way to the simple figure of the plain aisled rectangle. So the new church was built throughout to the breadth the transept had occupied, the lower part of the old tower retained, and its upperworks replaced by two new stages, which must have seemed to the onlookers, who attended the rededication ceremony in 1497, to give the whole building the final stamp of modernity. Even today it has that kind of look, as expressing a summing-up of all tower-design throughout the Middle Ages, with its parapet (quite revised) pierced by two large quatrefoils and its divided pinnacles, split, as it were, across the angle. Fairford is unique as the complete English parish church of the year 1500, almost the very last of the old Gothic line and of the *ancien regime*. At the foot of the effigies of the founder and his wife we read:

For Jesus' love, pray for me:
I may not pray, nowe pray ye,
With a Paternoster & an Ave,
That my paynys relessid may be.

Yet, within half a century, such prayers in church were to be ruled out of order.

Finchingfield, Essex

This East Anglian village, though widely distributed, is one of the least changed. It has several old houses of the better sort and still keeps its large village green and horse-pond, as seen in the picture. The horse-pond, once an almost universal amenity of every village, has become more rare than the village green. One of the pleasant early morning sounds in the country in earlier days (still remembered by many) was that of teamsters and waggoners passing down the village street with a jingling, clopping noise to "water their horses" at the communal pool. And there, too, often took place that interesting combined operation of black-smith and wheelwright, the shrinking on of an iron tyre to the rim of a wooden wheel—the dull red iron put on the smoking felloes and then the whole cast into the pond to cool quickly and contract. Less pleasant to remember was the "treatment" of scolds and suspected witches in these stagnant waters. Now the horse-pond, where it remains, is an unfailing delight to artist and photographer. Essex is particularly well off for greens, horse-ponds, and village pumps (of the authentic square box and long handle).

Denham, Buckinghamshire

Although only a few miles from London, and gradually becoming outflanked by urban enterprises and overflows, Denham still keeps the essential charm and character of an English village of the home counties. The house with Dutch gables (late seventeenth century, except the addition on the right) is reminiscent of the days of William and Mary and a very chaste and well-preserved example of that time.

Godstone, Surrey

Industrial encroachments have reached, and partly overwhelmed the old village but have been successfully resisted by the village green through time-honoured prescriptive rights. Such greens were once the scene of archery contests which were thought so much more important (in the national interest) than any other sport that, in the fourteenth century, by a law of Edward III, anyone chosing to play cricket there was liable to three years imprisonment. But by the nineteenth century things had so much changed that cricket had become the great national game, and village cricket was especially valued, not as a training for war but as a discipline for the newly conceived ideal of fair play.

The Bell Inn, Hurley, Berkshire

Hurley, in the Thames Valley, has several old half-timbered houses, of which the Bell is a fair sample. Its arrangement of gables suggests a pre-Elizabethan date. The sign was a popular one and must, in nearly every case, have referred to the church bell. It was also well chosen, as ringers were amongst the most reliable patrons of the village inn. Bell-ringing is thirsty work, and it is a very old grievance with the clergy that the men who summon the faithful to prayer neglect the refreshment of their own souls by stealing away from the ringing-chamber after the last pull of the rope to refresh their bodies at the inn with long pulls of another sort. In this case, the church was that of a priory which belonged to Westminster Abbey. Just before the dissolution of the monasteries, Henry VIII had bargained with those monks of Westminster to give them Hurley Wood in exchange for their convent garden (since corrupted to Covent Garden). The priory was acquired by the Lovelace family, who established themselves on the site, but the monastic church (and one of its mediaeval bells) remained in use by the parish. One cannot help wondering how the gossip ran in the local news-exchange (the Bell parlour) towards the end of the next century, that is, the month of June, 1688. Of course everyone would have heard what happened on the 10th, the birth of a prince in London—that was going to spoil the chances of Princess Mary of Orange and blight the hopes of all good Protestants. But then, on the last day of that month, had anyone seen an unknown Jack Tar rolling up the street of Hurley? If so, why hadn't he called at the usual resort particularly favoured by seamen? No! I believe that, even at the Bell, and even if they had seen this particularly able seaman not one know-all would have recognised under his tarred Brab hat the face of Admiral Herbert, 8th Earl of Pembroke, just come from Holland with an important communication from Prince William of Orange, or known that he was gone up to the Big House to confer with Lord Lovelace and other prominent Whigs, who intended to keep their meeting so secret that it was held in the charnel-house of the old Priory, where the remains of holy men still lay about. But that was what settled matters for King James and the new-born Prince, and brought William III to England.

Lower Brockhampton, Herefordshire

The old manor-house of the lords of Brockhampton retains its original hall which, when built in the fourteenth century, comprised the whole establishment. Later, when ideas of domestic comfort were more enlarged, a wing was built at right angles to provide separate bedrooms. The house is moated as a discouragement to thieves and robbers, which were common enough in the Border counties during the fourteenth and fifteenth centuries, but it was not fortified in any military sense. The gatehouse guarding the bridge on which it stands, is rather to emphasise the manorial dignity of the dwelling than for defensive purpose, though it is closed by a massive oaken door, heavily studded. Matching the house in half-timber construction it completes a delightfully picturesque group.

Audley End, Essex

The house is built on lands formerly belonging to the Benedictine Abbey of Walden. At the dissolution of the monasteries they were granted by Henry VIII to the most powerful and unscrupulous of all his ministers, Sir Thomas Audley. Through his daughter the property came to the Howard family, and Thomas Howard, 1st Duke of Suffolk and Lord High Treasurer of England, began to build in 1603, with the avowed intention of making Audley End the largest house in the realm. James I, who was entertained there in 1614 is said to have commented that the house "was too much for a king but might do well for a lord treasurer". What we see standing today is less than a quarter the size of that vast mansion. Formerly, the buildings were arranged about three courts, an immense one towards the river, a smaller in the rear of that, and a third, enclosed only on three sides, beyond that again. The front of the house which is seen in the picture formed the dividing range between the large court and the next and, as at Haddon Hall and Wingfield Manor, the great hall was situated here. It still occupies the ground floor between the two porticos—the upper floor was a much later addition. When the house was still intact it was acquired by Charles II as a palace, the Commonwealth interregnum having left him badly off for royal house-room. But, when William III acceded, there was £50,000 of the purchase-price still unpaid to the heir of the former owner, and the estate was re-granted to him (1701) in lieu of this deficit. By now, the huge palace was falling into decay and in 1720, on Vanburgh's advice, the great front court (measuring some 230 feet either way) was demolished. A little later, the third court and all the eastern side of the other (which contained the long gallery) was pulled down. One of the most interesting things about Audley End is its association with Magdalene College, Cambridge, where (through a link with the old monks of Walden Abbey) the right of presentation to the mastership of the college has always gone with the house, no matter who its owner might be.

Hampton Court Palace, Middlesex

Hampton Court is one of the two great houses which Cardinal Wolsey built for himself, the other being Whitehall where, however, nothing remains above ground of the work of his time: at Hampton Court there is still a great deal left. Here, the cardinal-chancellor is said to have employed 500 persons in his household and kept 280 rooms fully furnished and in constant readiness to receive guests. But, in 1528, on the eve of his fall, he tried to avert disaster by making a present of Hampton Court with all its costly contents to his master, King Henry VIII. Henry made some additions and replaced Wolsey's great hall with a larger and grander one. From then until 1688 the palace remained a typical great house of the early Tudor period, with its three quadrangles in brick, angle towers, and tall turreted gateways. Then William of Orange arrived. He had already ordered a new palace to be built at Kensington. In addition, he instructed Wren to rebuild Hampton Court. A beginning was made by converting the large block surrounding the eastern quadrangle to state apartments in the style of the time. The work was not quite finished in 1702, when the reign of William and Mary ended. So those sovereigns lived only in Kensington Palace and never occupied Hampton Court and all the new work, with furniture and fittings, was inherited by Queen Anne who spent much time here and made some additions. But the larger plan of rebuilding was never carried out and no sovereign since George II's time has lived there. The public is admitted to the gardens and the Wren state-rooms which are all on the first floor. Other floors are occupied by families who have been associated with distinguished service to the crown. The picture shows Wren's work on the east front (right) and south side, where the names of William and Mary appear over the central colonnade. It is much to be regretted that in 1771 Wolsey's imposing gatehouse at the principal entrance was shorn of its two upper floors. This kind of thing is not likely to happen again. The whole place is carefully preserved and kept in beautiful order by H.M. Ministry of Works.

Petworth House, Sussex

The manor of Petworth came into possession of the Percy family (whose larger estates, with the great castles of Warkworth and Alnwick lay in their earldom of Northumberland) in the twelfth century, and Petworth House is still inhabited by a descendant. The last to bear the ancient name was Elizabeth Percy who lived in the time of Charles II. Through her marriage all the estates passed to the Seymour Dukes of Somerset. In the next generation the claimants were two heiresses and the vast Percy inheritance was divided between the families into which they married—Smithsons and Wyndhams, the northern estates going to the former branch, which re-adopted the name of Percy and became Dukes of Northumberland, while Petworth remained with the Wyndhams. The present house was built by the Lady Elizabeth's husband, the 6th Duke of Somerset (though only married to him at the age of sixteen, he was her third husband). The building was begun in 1688 but is not associated with any well-known architect of the period. The picture shows the west front which faintly suggests the "three-piece" façade of a century earlier. It is 320 feet long but pleasantly unpretentious. Although Wren appears to have had nothing to do with the design his accompanist in woodwork, Grinling Gibbons, carried out one of his most ambitious embellishments in one of the great rooms, now called after his name. It is the interior, in fact, which gives the house its most striking character. It is enriched by a wonderful collection of pictures; for George Wyndham, who lived here at the end of the eighteenth century and the beginning of the nineteenth was a keen and knowledgeable connoisseur, a collector of pictures and a good friend to artists who stayed and worked here as his guests—Turner among many others. So here are gathered not only the interesting family portraits of the Percies but a tremendously well-stocked gallery of the Georgian masters. Only one room of the older house remains—the thirteenth-century chapel. The house was presented to the National Trust in 1947 by Mr. John Wyndham (who still lives there) and the pictures and furniture loaned.

West Wycombe Park, Buckinghamshire

This house (mainly of the second half of the eighteenth century) was the home of Sir Francis Dashwood (later, 15th Baron le Despenser) who, while constantly consulting architects and artists about the various additions he made from time to time and the elaborate decoration of the interior, always ended by going his own way. Dashwood is chiefly remembered for some of the most high-spirited frolics of "The Age of Reason" and for his part in the formation of a mock religious society called The Monks of Medmenham (to outsiders, the Hell Fire Club). He was, however, a consistently devoted patron of the arts and one of the foremost concerned in the foundation of the Dilettanti Society which, in its early days, did a notable service in giving financial support to the publication of Stuart and Revett's great work *The Antiquities of Athens, measured and delineated*, which was the immediate means of introducing the Neo-Grecian style of architecture to England. Revett, himself, was employed at West Wycombe Park on the Western Portico, carried out according to the new enlightenment in Greek Ionic. It is the East Portico (Roman Doric) which appears in the picture and South Front (a typical Palladian composition). It looks out towards West Wycombe Hill and the church, whose tower is surmounted by that immense copper globe (another frolicsome work of Sir Francis). The main entrance of the house is here; but, in order to display the whole edifice on every side to the arriving guest, the drive is made to take him in a wide sweep round to Revett's Ionic portico. A passage then conducts him out of the house again into the middle of the open loggia, where he will at last find the front door. Sir John Dashwood presented the house and grounds to the National Trust in 1944. Its interior fittings and decorations reflect the ambitious ideas of a rich man of taste of the time in which orthodoxy and innovation are mixed.

Magdalen Tower, Oxford

Magdalen tower stands detached from the college chapel in the range of buildings fronting on High Street. It was built at the very end of the fifteenth century and has a ring of ten bells of varying dates, the oldest older than the tower. It was one of the last works carried out in pure Perpendicular Gothic and, with its octagonal buttresses rising into tall turret-pinnacles and its ornate perforated battlements, shows the latest development which the evolution of mediaeval tower-design had reached. The tower stands 144 feet high. At sunrise on May morning the college choir ascends to the leads and sings, a custom which originated when the tower was first completed.

Magdalen College was founded by William of Waynflete, Bishop of Winchester and lord chancellor of England. Standing in its ample grounds and with its deer-park, it is one of the largest and most beautiful of the Oxford colleges.

In the foreground is Magdalen Bridge built by John Gwynn in 1772 (widened a century later). It carries the London road over the Cherwell, a branch of the Thames.

Broad Street, Oxford

The middle building (surmounted by a cupola) is the Sheldonian Theatre, so called because the cost of its erection was borne by Gilbert Sheldon, Archbishop of Canterbury and Chancellor of the University of Oxford. He was distressed that the ceremony of granting degrees and other academic occasions were still being held in St. Mary's Church—as they had been from earliest times, the University having no roomy building of its own for these purposes. Sir Christopher Wren was commissioned to design and carry out the plan which takes the form of a theatre of the classical age. He began the work in 1664. Wren was then Savilian Professor of Astronomy in the University and was interested in architecture only as one of his many intellectual diversions. He had, however, built a new chapel for Pembroke College, Cambridge; the Sheldonian Theatre was his second building.

The Theatre was intended to serve another purpose, that of housing the University Press. This was provided for between the auditorium and the roof. The floor which had a span of 80 feet had to withstand the weight of the heavy printing-presses and was designed with great scientific skill on a principal of dovetailed rafters held rigid by wooden girders. The Press was, however, moved into the Clarendon Building (seen on the left) which was specially designed for it by Nicholas Hawksmoor, completed in 1715. It is so named because it was mainly built from the proceeds of Lord Clarendon's *History of the Great Rebellion*, the profits of which his son presented to the University. Thus derives the famous name of the Clarendon Press, removed once again in 1830 to its present quarters in Walton Street.

The building on the right is the modern range of Exeter College.

The Backs, Cambridge

The *Backs*, those park-like grounds with umbrageous walks, lawns, gardens, and wildernesses, which face their owner colleges across the river, constitute one of the most individual features of Cambridge. The picture shows such a cared-for wilderness at the far end of Queens' Backs, though that college is out of sight behind the photographer.

The building on the right is the end of River Court, King's College, an addition carried out in 1893 by G. F. Bodley. There intervenes the wide lawn (over which the famous group of King's Chapel and the Fellows' Building* is shot by floating camera-men a thousand times a year) and then Clare College is seen. It is a foundation of 1326, but this handsome and distinctive building (all the work of three masons, John Westley, Thomas and Robert Grumbold) was not begun till 1638. But after the beginning of the Civil War all the stone and materials carefully got together for the work were commandeered by the Parliamentary forces to be wastefully scattered in defence works of the town, and it was not until 1715 that the building was finished.

Through the single arch of King's Bridge appears that of Clare (by Thomas Grumbold in 1638) though the stone balls on the parapet are not seen. To be set to count these used to be a test for stability after a wine party. But it is really a mathematical problem for sober wranglers, as one ball has lost a slice of its rotundity and the correct answer must be in fractions or decimals.

* The old familiar name. Now it is called simply "Gibbs" after the architect who designed it.

Trinity College, Cambridge

The picture shows the east range of Great Court with the principal entrance, the Great Gate. The college chapel is on the left, and the fountain stands near the middle of the court. Great Court is an immense quadrangle which gives the impression of having been first designed as now seen. That is far from being the case. It was created out of a single demolition of three irregular courts with assorted buildings which had, so to speak, thrown themselves together when the two venerable and neighbouring colleges of King's Hall and Michaelhouse had been, in the same year (1546), dissolved and refounded as Trinity College by Henry VIII.

To make one fine harmonious architectural conception out of the mediaeval hotch-potch was the bold venture of the Master who reigned at the end of the sixteenth century, Thomas Nevile; his energy, good taste, and long purse enabled him to carry it out. The two earlier colleges, just named, were foundations of the early fourteenth century. The Great Gate, whose position was not disturbed by the wholesale demolitions, was a late addition to King's Hall and only completed in 1519. The three figures, however, which can be seen standing in their niches over the archway were put there by Nevile and represent James I, his Queen, and Prince Charles. The fountain is also a work of Nevile placed last, like a decorative full-stop to the first and greatest of his three achievements in remodelling and enlarging his college. But it plays from a lead pipeline laid from a source two miles away and beyond the river by the Franciscan friars in the year 1327 to supply their house with running water.

Between the Great Gate and the chapel is seen the entrance to the staircase leading to Sir Isaac Newton's old rooms.

The Shakespeare Memorial Theatre, Stratford-on-Avon, Warwickshire

The idea of honouring the memory of Shakespeare by a national festival, held in the town where he was born and died, originated with his great exponent, the actor, David Garrick, who held a Shakespeare jubilee at Stratford-on-Avon in 1769. Thus started, this commemorative ceremony was repeated from time to time in later years and, eventually, became an annual festival, timed to take place in the week which included Shakespeare's birthday—April the 23rd. The aims of the Festival were focused in 1877 by the formation of a Shakespeare Association whose energies were directed towards raising a more substantial background to the cult by the erection of a permanent building to embody a full-sized theatre where the plays could be performed in the Festival week, also a library and picture-gallery devoted to collections of Shakespeariana. This, the Shakespeare Memorial, designed in modern Gothic by W. F. Unsworth, was opened in 1879, but completely destroyed by fire in 1926, the other buildings of the Memorial with their valuable collections (including the Droeshout portrait of Shakespeare) escaping unhurt. The theatre was rebuilt to designs by Elizabeth Scott, grand-niece of the famous Gothic revivalist, Sir Gilbert. But neither he nor Unsworth did she follow. She was modern in her treatment, both outside and in, where room is even provided for a rolling-stage. The Memorial is here seen from the left bank of the River Avon.